Chakra Clearing

Chakra Clearing

Awakening Your Spiritual Power to Know and Heal

Doreen Virtue, Ph.D.

HAY
HOUSE

HAY HOUSE, INC.
Carlsbad, California • New York City
London • Sydney • Johannesburg
Vancouver • New Delhi

Copyright © 1998 by Doreen Virtue

Published and distributed in the United States by: Hay House, Inc.: www.hay house.com • *Published and distributed in Australia by:* Hay House Australia Pty. Ltd.: www.hayhouse.com.au • *Published and distributed in the United Kingdom by:* Hay House UK, Ltd.: www.hayhouse.co.uk • *Published and distributed in the Republic of South Africa by:* Hay House SA (Pty), Ltd.: www.hayhouse.co.za • *Distributed in Canada by:* Raincoast: www.raincoast.com • *Published in India by:* Hay House Publishers India: www.hayhouse.co.in

Edited by: Jill Kramer   *Designed by:* Wendy Lutge

The author of this book does not dispense medical advice or prescribe the use of any technique as a form of treatment for physical or medical problems without the advice of a physician, either directly or indirectly. The intent of the author is only to offer information of a general nature to help you in your quest for emotional and spiritual well-being. In the event you use any of the information in this book for yourself, which is your constitutional right, the author and the publisher assume no responsibility for your actions.

Library of Congress Cataloging-in-Publication Data

Virtue, Doreen.
    Chakra clearing : awakening your spiritual power to know and heal / Doreen Virtue.
        p.   cm.
      ISBN 1-56170-566-7 (pbk.)
      1. Chakras—Miscellanea.   I. Title.
  BF1442.C53V57   1998
  131—dc21   98-30403
                                      CIP

ISBN 13: 978-1-56170-566-5
ISBN 10: 1-56170-566-7

10 09 08 07 21 20 19 18
1st printing, November 1998
18th printing, September 2007

Printed in the United States of America

Contents

Introduction

You Are a Being of Light

*Y*ou are a being composed of light, love, and intelligence. These characteristics are the essence of pure energy. So, you are an energetic being. Sometimes, though, you may not feel that way. In fact, you might feel the complete *opposite* of energy. Still, you have unlimited energy within you right now, and this energy has remarkable gifts.

Your thoughts control the energy flow within and around you. Whatever you think about determines how you feel and what you experience. Different energy centers within and around your body are influenced by your thinking habits. In other words, the things you concentrate on the most—money, spirituality, relationships, and so on—affect your energy centers. These energy centers look like fans, with their blades overlapping. We call them "chakras" (pronounced *SHOCK-RUHS*), which means "wheel" in the ancient Eastern language of Sanskrit.

Although the body has many chakras, psychics and healers generally only concern themselves with the *major* ones. These chakras are each found next to a hormonal gland. They push vital life energy (also called "ki," "chi," or "prana") through the body to ensure vitality. They're like pinball-game paddles pushing balls along their course. This life energy springs from the Divine and gives us access to all wisdom, or psychic information.

Your chakras radiate and receive energy constantly. If you hold negative thoughts, your chakras become dirty with dense, dark energy. Dirty chakras can't push through sufficient energy, and you feel sluggish and out of balance. You also lose touch with your natural psychic abilities.

You have a chakra for each "issue" that you commonly think about. There's a chakra related to thoughts about money and career, relationships, your future, appetite and lifestyle habits, and goals and aspirations. If you completely base your thoughts in love and faith, these chakras operate at a perfectly healthy rate. Your energy and life flow smoothly, and you experience harmony and bliss.

However, almost everyone is prone to worrying or obsessing about life occasionally. Fear thoughts affect the chakra, that corresponds to the issue you are thinking about. That particular chakra then becomes dirty, shrunken, or swollen. Consequently, you may experience fatigue or listlessness without realizing why.

Your chakras also affect your intuitive abilities. With cleansed and balanced chakras, you can easily discern information about your future and about other people, and hear the voices of God and the angels.

In this book, you will learn the functions of the major chakras, and esoteric methods for clearing them of fear. Your natural state is one of high energy, intuition, and creativity. You don't need to add anything to yourself to enjoy these characteristics—you already own them within yourself. Just like a sculptor needs to chip away the parts of the statue that aren't part of the ultimate creation, you only need to clear away fear to reveal your innate qualities.

Chapter One

The Functions of Your Chakras

*Y*ou have hundreds of chakras within and around you. In fact, every living being, including the earth, has chakras. Let's focus on the major chakras that affect your daily life. These are located deep within the center of your physical body. The chakras in the lower part of your body spin slower than those in your upper body and head. Also, your lower chakras correspond to issues of the material world, while your upper chakras are focused upon more spiritual issues.

Chakras spin in a clockwise direction. Imagine yourself looking at a spinning oscillator fan, similar to the silver ventilating fans you see on top of industrial buildings. While you're looking directly *at* a person, their chakras appear as fans that you're seeing from the side. From above, their chakras would look like an aerial view of spinning fans.

Just as slow-moving light waves appear as warm hues of color, so do the lower and slower chakras appear in shades of red, orange, and yellow. The upper chakras, which spin faster, have cool shades of green, blue, violet, and purple. Once you clear your chakras, you will reawaken your ability to see chakras within your own body and within others. In addition, you can see auras, as explained a little later in this book.

The Root Chakra

Located at the base of your spine, the *root* chakra spins at the slowest rate of all the major chakras. Its slow rate creates a brilliant ruby-red color. When the root chakra is clean, it sparkles with white crystal lights, mingled with a rich, clear shade of red. A clear root chakra looks like a brilliant ruby held under a bright spotlight. However, when it gets dirty, the root chakra has a muddy, dark red color to it.

Your root chakra is related to issues of physical security and is affected by your thoughts and feelings about:

- *Finances*: money, savings, bills, retirement accounts, the economy, gambling, the lottery, and finances.

- *Career*: making enough money, being in the "right" job for you, issues of benefits and retirement, commuting, concerns about layoffs or promotions, and thoughts about your future.

- *Home*: desires to move, feelings of safety, the condition and energy of your home, the arrangement of items in your home (Feng Shui), maintaining your home, and thoughts about buying a home.

- *Physical Safety*: feeling safe or unsafe.

- *Needs*: having enough to eat, and sufficient clothing for yourself and your loved ones.

- *Possessions*: vehicles, furniture, jewelry, and work-related equipment.

Fears related to having your physical needs met make your root chakra shrink in size and grow dark and dirty. You literally choke your root chakra with worries about money, career, or possessions. This creates feelings of lack and limitation, as if there's "never enough to go around." A clogged root chakra usually creates self-fulfilling prophecies involving money challenges.

Obsessions about money, career, and possessions—the workaholic mind-set—create a dirty root chakra that is extremely large. Now, there's nothing wrong with having a large root chakra. In fact, we will work later in this book to enlarge all of your chakras. The only problem is when your chakras are all different sizes. Obsessions create imbalances, because they make one or more chakras bigger than the other chakras. Chakra clearing helps you balance all of your chakras so that they are equally large and clean.

Sacral Chakra

The second major root chakra is found midway between your navel and the base of your spine. The *sacral* (pronounced *SAY-KRULL*) chakra spins slightly faster than the red root chakra, so it appears as a beautiful shade of orange. A balanced and clear sacral chakra glows with a pale, clean white interior. A dirty sacral chakra has a burnt orange coloring.

The sacral chakra is affected by your thoughts and feelings with respect to:

- *Cravings for physical pleasures*: food, drink, sex, or thrill-seeking.

- *Addictions*: drugs, alcohol, food, and other substances.

- *Your body*: exercise habits, sleep patterns, weight, health, and thoughts about your appearance.

If you are worried or stressed about any issue concerning your body, your sacral chakra will appear shrunken and dirty. You may experience fatigue or listlessness as a result. On the other hand, if you are obsessed with your body, your sacral chakra will look dirty and oversized. Again, there is nothing wrong with having a large chakra. We just want to make sure that all of your chakras are clean and equal in size.

Solar Plexus Chakra

The third major chakra, called the *solar plexus* chakra, is found right behind the navel. This chakra spins at a faster rate than the root and the sacral chakras, so it appears in shades of bright yellow. A clean and balanced solar plexus chakra looks like a ball of sunshine, with yellow and bright white sparkling light. When a solar plexus chakra gets dirty, it appears as a muddy shade of yellow, mixed with patches of brown and black.

The solar plexus chakra is affected by thoughts and feelings about:

- *Power*: the fear of being, or desire to be, a powerful person; fear of authority figures; obsessions with power; concerns about people or nations that wield a lot of power; current or past experiences in which you felt overpowered by another person.

- *Control*: fears of being controlled by others; fear of losing control; desires for control over yourself, situations, or other people; current or past experiences in which you felt controlled or out of control.

If you fear that others are trying to over-power or control you, then your solar plexus chakra will appear dark yellow and small. If you have obsessions about *gaining* power and control, your solar plexus chakra will enlarge and look muddy yellow in color.

During the chakra clearing exercises described in this book, you can release fears or obsessions from the solar plexus and your other chakras.

Heart Chakra

We call the fourth major chakra, located in the center of the chest, the *heart* chakra. This chakra represents the beginning of the upper chakras, which all correspond to spiritual issues. The lower chakras are primarily concerned with physical and material issues. The heart chakra, which spins at a medium-fast speed, is a beautiful shade of green. A cleansed and balanced heart chakra looks like a brilliant emerald jewel, sparkling under a bright white spotlight. A dirty heart chakra appears dark forest green in color.

The heart chakra is affected by thoughts and feelings concerning:

- *Relationships*: with mother, father, step-parents, grandparents, siblings, and other family members; past lovers or spouses; friends; co-workers; employers; teachers; strangers; and peers.

- *Love*: Divine love from God and your higher self; romantic, platonic, and familial love.

- *People attachments*: codependency, dysfunctional relationship addictions, or obsessions about a person.

- *Forgiveness or unforgiveness*: toward oneself; another person (living, deceased, famous, friend, or family member); or toward a country, group of people, governmental agency, or organization.

Any fears about receiving or giving love will shrink and dirty the heart chakra. Relationship addictions and obsessions create an enlarged and clogged heart chakra. In either case, an unclear heart chakra prevents a person from experiencing the deep bliss of true love.

Just about everyone has some fears about experiencing true communion and intimacy with another person, primarily because most individuals have experienced pain in a love relationship. As a result, we eventually associate love with pain. We then create barriers in our heart chakra to prevent ourselves from losing control and feeling love deeply (lest we be hurt again). However, our Divine origin is spiritual love. Love is the source of all of our power, of everything we need and desire. To block love's awareness is to block *everything*. In the chakra-clearing work that follows, we'll work with the angelic realm to heal these fears.

The heart chakra is a central component in the development of your intuition or clairsentience, which means "clear feeling."

The more we cleanse and open our heart chakras, the greater intensity and accuracy our clairsentience has.

Throat Chakra

The fifth major chakra is in the Adam's apple area and is called the *throat* chakra. It spins at a fast rate and is sky-blue in color. A clean throat chakra looks like a sparkling clear sunshiny day, while a dirty throat chakra looks like a dreary, dismal day.

The throat chakra is affected by thoughts and feelings related to:

- *Speaking your truth to*: yourself, your loved ones, acquaintances, your clients and customers, co-workers and employers, and your audiences.

- *Communication projects*: involving singing, writing, speaking, artistic works, channeling, and teaching other people.

- *Asking for your needs to be met*: by God, your loved ones, your employers and co-workers, and yourself.

Fears about communicating shrink the throat chakra and often create physical discomfort in that area. Obsessions about communicating can overstimulate your throat chakra, resulting in an imbalanced and disproportionately large chakra.

Ear Chakras

The sixth and seventh chakras are inside your head, just above your left and right ears. Resting at a 30-degree angle, the *ear* chakras radiate a beautiful shade of reddish-violet. Clean ear chakras look like sparkling maroon jewels, mingled with flashes of white and pale violet. Dirty ear chakras look opaque, with no light coming through them. They are muddy and dark colored.

The ear chakras relate to your thoughts and feelings about:

- *Divine communication*: your reluctance or desire to hear the voice of God and the spiritual realm.

- *What you hear or have heard*: mentally replaying loving or fear-based phrases in your mind, unforgiveness toward someone who seems to have verbally abused you, negative or positive messages that you have picked up from the media, the content and energy of music, and noises in your environment.

Ear chakras are an important element in developing clairaudience, which means "clear hearing." Clairaudience allows you to clearly hear the voice of God, your higher self, angels, and ascended masters such as Jesus, Quan Yin, Buddha, Moses, Krishna, and Mohammed. Ear chakras most often become clogged if we hold unforgiveness toward a person who said something that felt painful to hear. They also become dark, dirty, and shrunken if we fear hearing God's guidance for any reason.

Third Eye

The eighth major chakra is between the two eyes. We often call it the *brow* or the *ajna* (pronounced *AHZH-NAH*) chakra. However, we most commonly call it the *third eye*, and for good reason. If you close your eyes, take a few deep breaths, and place your attention on the area between your two physical eyes, you will begin to see or feel an oval-shaped object lying on its side. This is your third eye, and it is looking directly at you. It is the eye of your true self or your higher self. The reason why the eye is turned toward you is because everything is within you. There is nothing else except what is in your heart and mind. It is only an illusion that a material world exists outside of and separate from you.

Your third eye records a movie of your entire life, including everything you think, feel, and do. It also records all of the emotions felt by everyone with whom you come in contact. After you pass on to the other side, you will watch this movie during a life review.

The third eye is a little different from the other chakras because of the eye in its center. Surrounding the eye is an energy center radiating a deep color of indigo blue, with sparkles of white and flashes of purple lights.

The third eye chakra is affected by thoughts and feelings relating to:

- *The future*: your desire or reluctance to clearly see what is in store for you.

- *The past*: if a vision that you had frightened you, or if you were persecuted in this life or a past one for being psychic (psychics were frequently killed for being "witches" in past times; and children who are told that psychic abilities and clairvoyance are "evil" often shut their third eyes).

- *Beliefs about spirits*: your desire to see, or fear of seeing, angels or apparitions.

When the third eye chakra is cleansed, you will see the eye of your higher self clearly looking at you. Seeing an eyelid over the third eye signifies a closed third eye. This eyelid may be completely shut, partially open, or blinking open and shut. Or, the third eye could have a screen over it, blocking full spiritual vision.

Crown Chakra

The ninth major chakra is found near the inside of the top of the head, and it looks like a ceiling fan colored in vivid royal purple. The *crown* chakra crowns the chakras within our bodies. It is essential to claircognizance, or "clear knowing," which is the ability to receive thoughts, information, and ideas from the Divine mind or collective unconscious. Those who are highly claircognizant can tap into the wealth of creativity and inventions that abound in the spiritual plane.

The crown chakra is affected by thoughts and feelings relating to:

- *God*: whether we feel close, estranged from, indifferent to, or angry at our Creator.

- *Religion or spirituality*: if we have had negative experiences with formal religion, our anger or unforgiveness can clog our crown chakra.

- *Divine guidance*: our feelings about receiving direction or ideas from the universal Source. Some people are threatened by the idea of "someone" telling them what to do, even if this someone is God or the collective unconscious.

- *Trust*: our willingness or unwillingness to receive information or facts from the etheric plane, without knowing "how" we know.

A clean crown chakra glows in a beautiful, rich shade of purple, interspersed with sparkles of diamond-white light. Crown chakras clogged with unhealed emotions and bitter thoughts about Divine guidance, God, or negative religious experiences look as dark as the night sky. Fortunately, the chakras respond quickly to cleansing techniques such as those described later in this book.

CHAKRA CHART

←— Crown Chakra
←— Ear Chakras
←— Third Eye

←— Throat Chakra

←— Heart Chakra

←— Solar Plexus Chakra

←— Sacral Chakra

←— Root Chakra

Here is a summary of the names, locations, functions, and colors of the major chakras:

THE MAJOR CHAKRAS

CHAKRA	LOCATION
Crown	Inside the top of the head
Third eye	Between the eyes
Ear chakras	Above the physical ears, inside the head
Throat	Adam's apple
Heart	Chest
Solar plexus	Stomach area
Sacral	3 to 4 inches below the solar plexus
Root	Base of spine

CORRESPONDING ISSUES	COLOR
Claircognizance and Divine guidance	Royal purple
Clairvoyance	Dark blue
Clairaudience	Red-violet
Communication, speaking your truth	Light blue
Love, realization of oneness	Emerald green
Power and control	Yellow
Physical desires and appetites, addictions	Orange
Survival and sustenance concerns, such as money, shelter, and basic material needs	Red

Chapter Two

Meditations to Clear Your Chakras

*A*lmost every day we have fear-based thoughts. We frequently encounter people or situations that inspire fear of some kind. Consequently, we may absorb fearful energy into our chakras. For that reason, it's a good idea to clear your chakras every day. Just as you bathe and wash your face daily, so does your energy body benefit from consistent cleansing.

Chakra clearing involves two steps:

1. *Clearing*: releasing negative thought-forms and etheric cords from our chakras; and

2. *Balancing*: enlarging the chakras so that they are all the same size.

Chakras shrink in size when we hold fearful thoughts about the issues corresponding to the shrunken chakra. They enlarge out of proportion to the other chakras when we have obsessions about the issue related to a particular one. For example, fears about money would create a shrunken root chakra. Obsessions about acquiring money would create a disproportionately large one.

There is nothing inherently wrong with having a large chakra; in fact, it is healthy. We just need to keep them equally large so that energy flows through them without interruption.

Dirty or imbalanced chakras result in feelings of lethargy, fatigue, and apparent blocks in one's creativity and flow of abundance. Clean and balanced chakras open up our flow of energy, new ideas, and synchronicities.

There are dozens of methods to clear your chakras, and I am grateful that so many options are available to us. It's enjoyable to be able to vary our chakra-cleansing routine. If I'm in a hurry, I'll use the shorter methods, and then reserve the thorough and lengthy methods for times when I have an open schedule.

In this book, I will describe several of my favorite methods. I encourage you to try each of them so you will have experiences with them in your repertoire. Then, of course, you'll use whichever method feels most efficient and comfortable.

Probably the method most widely used to clear chakras is meditation. I use the following meditation for myself, my students, and clients. It is also recorded, with background music, by angelologist/pianist Randall Leonard on my audiocassette *Chakra Clearing* (Hay House, 1997).

These meditations are 12 and 15 minutes each in length. I have found that most of us can fit this amount of time into our busy schedules. There is a morning meditation, which starts the day off on a bright note with positive and empowering intentions. Then, the evening meditation clears away any negative energy that you may have absorbed during the day, and invokes angels into your dreams.

Basic Meditation Guidance

If you haven't meditated before, here are some guidelines to help you. Of course, your most important source of instruction in meditating—or for doing *anything*, for that matter—is your inner guidance. Do what comes naturally, and you'll be following the ultimate authority.

First, find a quiet place where you can be alone or where others won't interrupt your thoughts. This could be a corner of your bedroom, a bathroom, your garden, a park, or even your automobile. Next, sit comfortably. There's no need to contort your legs in uncomfortable postures; inner peace isn't "hard-won." Instead, sit in whatever position feels natural to you. Then, either close your eyes or look down to block out visual distractions.

After that, take two or three extremely deep breaths. Breathe in through your mouth, and breathe out through your nose. As you inhale, hold your breath for a few seconds, and then exhale thoroughly.

As you meditate, your lower-self or "ego" may try to distract you. It does this because it is afraid that you will find peace of mind. If you are centered in peacefulness and are unafraid, then the ego loses all of its power to control you with fear. So, the ego will bombard your mind with thoughts about trivia, bills, traffic, conflicts, or your body. It's important not to fight the ego or get angry with it. Anger gives the ego reality and power. In truth, it is nothing but a nightmarish illusion.

So, if you have a fear-based thought while meditating, simply notice it and then release it. You can release it by visualizing the fearful thought as a soap bubble, and then seeing yourself hand this soap bubble to your guardian angel. Or, you can visualize shining your inner Divine light on the fearful thought, and watch it disappear. You can also breathe out the fearful thought, and breathe in a replacement thought of love and true power.

During the meditations that follow, you'll read many affirmations that deal with releasement. You'll notice that a common element in these affirmations is, "I am willing to release…" These affirmations are extremely effective.

If you are willing to release disempowering thoughts, and if you hold the intention of being centered in peaceful power, then your success is assured. The angels tell me repeatedly, "Your experiences are created by your intentions." If we are willing to release a negative mind-set, then the negativity is easily and rapidly released. We need only be *willing* to heal, and it is done.

After centering yourself in a comfortable place with a peaceful mind, read or listen to the chakra-clearing meditations for the morning and evening:

MORNING CHAKRA-CLEARING MEDITATION

Breathe in and out very deeply, as you begin to open up to the healing energy of your Divine light. You are perfect, whole, and complete, and you needn't add anything to yourself to experience your true power. You merely need to release a few blocks that bar you from fully experiencing and enjoying your true Divinity. Awaken to your spiritual power to heal yourself, your loved ones, and any situation in which you seem to find yourself. Fully awaken to your gifts of psychic insights, as you are a holy child of the infinite wisdom.

Let's begin by focusing your awareness on the Divine spark of crystal-white light, sparkling within the center of your stomach area. See or feel this white spark of light, shining like a pilot light within you. This is the spark of your true essence, your shining flame from God. Through your decision and intention, you can increase the size of this Divine light now. See or feel the Divine light expand in you instantly, filling your entire body and aura with the illumined flame of Divinity. Feel the warmth within you, filling you completely with love and peaceful energy.

Now, let's move your attention to the area at the base of your spine. See or feel an illumined red circle, whirling in a clockwise direction. The circle looks like a spinning fan with overlapping fan blades. It glows a beautiful shade of ruby red. This is your root chakra, the energy center connected to your thoughts and beliefs concerning money and physical security.

*Mentally see or feel your root chakra, checking for any areas of darkness in or around it, which fears and worries have brought about. It's normal for all of us to have these feelings and we needn't judge them; we just need to release them to our holy light for cleansing, purification, and transmutation. As you breathe in and out very deeply, ask the inner light of your holy spirit to cleanse and dissolve all darkness from your root chakra by saying, "**I allow the Light to dissolve away all fears, worries, and concerns related to money, security, and safety.**"*

See and feel your root chakra completely cleansed, illumined, and perfectly enlarged with Divine white light. Take in a very deep cleansing

breath and affirm, **"I know that I am perfectly
protected in all ways, and that all of my needs
are met and provided for at every moment."**

After taking another deep breath, bring your
attention to an area about four inches above your
root chakra. See or feel an orange circle, spinning
like a beautifully illuminated orange fan. You are
now scanning your sacral chakra, the energy center connected with your thoughts and beliefs concerning appetites and desires. Scan for any areas
of darkness in your sacral chakra, which you may
have absorbed from fearful thoughts.

Release and cleanse all traces of fear and
darkness to your holy spirit of Divine light by saying, **"I willingly release all my desires and
appetites to the Light, and allow them to
become perfectly aligned with the one beautiful
will of my higher self and God."**

Take in a very deep cleansing breath and
affirm: **"I am harmoniously aligned with the
ceaseless flow of supply and love that springs
from the golden fountain of light within my
center. All of my desires are perfectly balanced, now."**

After taking another deep breath, move your attention to your stomach area. There you'll find a beautiful spinning yellow circle that looks like a small beautiful sun. This is your solar plexus chakra, the energy center connected with your thoughts and beliefs concerning power and control. See or feel any areas of darkness within the yellow circle that may have come from any fears. As you take a deep cleansing breath, release all darkness and fear to your holy spirit and Divine light by saying, **"I release any fears or struggles concerning my power and control to the beautiful healing light within me. I have perfect power and control, now."**

See or feel your solar plexus perfectly cleansed and balanced, as you affirm: **"I graciously accept and fearlessly activate all of my power, now. This power, which is the power of oneness with God and all of creation, has pure motivations to love and to serve all of life. I create a beautifully loving and harmonious day for myself, and all of my interactions with others today come from this place of loving power."**

After taking another deep breath, move your attention to the heart area. Here you will see or feel a beautiful glowing emerald green circle, spinning like a fan made of luminescent jade. This is your heart chakra, the energy center connected with your thoughts and beliefs concerning love and relationships. Scan your chakra, with your inner vision or through your feeling, for any areas of darkness brought about by fear. As soon as you detect any darkness, notice it without any judgment, and simply release it to your holy spirit and Divine light by saying, "I am willing to release any fears that I have about receiving and giving love, now. I ask my holy spirit and light eternal to cleanse away all blocks that keep me from fully enjoying my love."

Now, take a very deep cleansing breath and affirm: "I now fully allow myself to give and receive Love. I am safe, and I am loved. I AM LOVED. I LOVE. I Love, I Love, I Love, I Love."

After taking another deep breath, move your attention to the throat area, where you will see or feel a beautiful, light blue spinning circle. This is your throat chakra, the energy center concerned with your thoughts and beliefs about spoken or written communication. If you have been afraid to speak your truth lately, you will probably now see or feel dark patches in your throat chakra. Let's release all fear blocks to communication with your Divine light by saying, "I willingly release any blocks to perfect communication to the light, now. I release all fear that would prevent me from lovingly speaking my truth today."

Then, take a refreshingly deep breath and affirm: "I allow my higher self and holy spirit to speak through me today, in all my communications. I step back and let Spirit lead the way, and all of my communications are perfectly ordered and guided. Today, everyone with whom I come in contact benefits from listening to my words."

Take another deep breath. Now focus on the area just above your ears and inside your head. Here you'll see or feel two spinning red-violet fans, with their blades overlapping, resting at a 30-degree angle inside the head, just above the left ear and the right ear. These are your ear chakras, the areas that regulate your ability to clearly hear the voice of God and the spiritual realm. If you have been having difficulty hearing the still, small voice within, you will probably notice that your ear chakras are dimly colored.

Let's brighten them up with your deep breath and focus on the Divine light within. With your decision and intention, you can now bring the white light into your left ear chakra and your right ear chakra. Watch as the light dissolves old fears connected with your spiritual hearing. As you breathe deeply, affirm, **"I am willing to release any fears I may have about hearing the voice of God, my higher self, the angels, and the Divine spiritual realm, now. I am willing to release any unforgiveness I may be holding toward anyone who ever said anything that I heard as a painful statement."**

Then, take a very deep breath and affirm as you breathe out: **"I now clearly hear, accept, and follow the guidance that comes to me for my highest and best good. I work in perfect partnership with the voice of Spirit, now and always."**

After taking another deep breath, move your focus to the area between your two eyes. Using your inner vision, allow yourself to see a spin-

ning circle of dark blue, which occasionally flashes white and purple sparkles of light. As you look at this circle, you may notice an oval shape in front of you, resting horizontally. This is your third eye, your window of clairvoyance and spiritual vision. Ask your third eye to fully open its eyelid so that you may fully see in truth and clarity. Take a deep breath and release all blocks to spiritual vision by saying, **"I am willing to release the fear of seeing the future. I am willing to release all fear of seeing the truth."**

And with another deep breath, anchor your new spiritual vision with this affirmation: **"I am safe as I allow my higher self to see the truth. My vision is perfectly ordered and illuminated by love."**

Take another deep breath, and move your attention to the area just inside the top of your head. This is your crown chakra, the energy center connected with your higher self and the universal all-knowing Mind. See or feel a majestic purple circle, spinning like a beautifully exotic ceiling fan at the dome of a skylight. If you sense any areas of fear or darkness in your crown chakra, you can cleanse them now by saying,

"I now allow the light of my holy spirit to dissolve away all barriers to Divine wisdom and guidance. I release all fear about listening to my higher self, God, and the angels."

Take another deep breath and affirm: "I know that I am perfectly safe as I follow my inner spiritual guidance. I allow this guidance to lead me to beautiful opportunities where I share my true nature as a powerful, loving, spiritual being. I listen, I trust, and take guided action. I listen. I trust. I take guided action. I trust."

Now you are fully illuminated and ready for an exciting day where your spiritual wisdom is fully awakened and activated. As you take deep breaths throughout your day, your energy will be continually recharged, and your chakras will be rebalanced and cleansed.

Let's give thanks to God, your angels, and your holy spirit for your awakened spiritual power, and affirm that it is right for you to be fully immersed in the warm glowing beauty of your true self. You are perfect, whole, and complete. And you are very, very loved!

∽✑

Evening Meditation

During this peaceful time of self-caring, your breaths and thoughts are now centered upon releasing and cleansing the day's events and preparing for a restful night's sleep. You deserve this time of respite and relaxation. Your mind willingly follows your intentions to focus upon the healing energy of the love that is within you, now.

Now it's time to fully cleanse and balance your root chakra—you may want to take several deep, cleansing breaths. With each breath that you take in, feel yourself becoming more and more relaxed and peaceful. With each exhalation, allow yourself to blow out any concerns you may have connected to your day. Be willing to release any cares or worries you may be holding in your cellular memory or in your auric field.

See and feel your root chakra at the base of your spine as a beautifully cleansed ruby-red fan, illumined and glowing with the brilliant light of your Divine spirit.

Affirm: **"All of my needs have already been provided to me. God is the Source Who perfect-**

ly provides for all of my physical needs, and I graciously accept this good into my life, now. I am safe, and I am loved."

As you continue to breathe in and out very deeply, you may notice that all of your internal organs begin to relax and you feel wonderfully blissful inside and outside. It's a good idea to now become willing to continue to release any remaining barriers that keep you from fully enjoying your Divine true essence. Be willing to release all of your goals, desires, and aspirations to the healing light within, knowing that as you do so, all of your needs are aligned into perfect harmony. Be willing to allow the light to dissolve any feelings of fear or guilt that may be blocking you from fully manifesting your Divine life purpose, now.

See and feel your sacral chakra, four inches above your root chakra, as a perfect orange jewel, glowing in intense white light. Affirm: *"I now fully accept my inner guidance as to my Divine life purpose, and I know that my will is totally aligned with God's will for my perfect happiness. I accept all of His support in manifesting my beautiful life mission into form.*

Now mentally review and release all of the interactions you had with other people today. Give everything over to your angels, your holy spirit, and to God so that you are free and completely unburdened. Allow yourself to admit your feelings to yourself, without censure or judgment. Then let them go, and know that by simply admitting any mistakes that were made today, they are purified and transmuted for everyone's growth and highest good. Mistakes simply require correction, not punishment, so you now willingly allow the growth lessons to come to you in perfect and Divine order.

If you have a sense that anyone is draining your energy, mentally cut the etheric psychic cord between you and the other person. Be willing to forgive that other person for seemingly draining you, and release the other person fully to the light, now. Completely let go of focusing on personalities of other people and ourselves, and focus, instead, on the true oneness of your spirit within the heart of God.

As you release all focus on personalities and seemingly separate bodies, see and feel your solar plexus chakra becoming purer and brighter until it glows like a beautiful little sun on a perfect spring morning. If you feel any sense that another person has irritated or angered you today, use this healing affirmation: **"I am willing to release that part of me that irritates me when I think of you."**

Then take a deep breath and affirm: **"Everyone in my life shares my goal in enjoying perfect love. I am blended with the one spirit who is the truth of every being whom God created. I am one, one, one with all of life—and I give thanks for this truth."**

Now ask for the Archangel Michael to surround your heart with his healing energy and to escort any darkness away from your heart. The angels live in a dimension unconstricted by time and space, so they are able to be with many, many people in different places simultaneously. Simply by asking for Michael's help and protection, he instantly appears by your side. Be willing to release any darkness, heaviness, or unforgiveness to the Archangel Michael so that he may take it to the light for purification and transmutation.

See or feel your heart chakra basking in the warm, glowing light of God's love. See your heart chakra as a beautiful emerald green glowing circle, spinning so perfectly and so smoothly. Affirm: **"I am willing to forgive myself and others for any mistakes in thinking, which were made during this day. I choose peace of mind in exchange for releasing these errors in thought. I ask that all effects of these errors be forgotten in all of time by all concerned."**

After a deep breath, see or feel yourself embraced and encircled by a loving group of angels. Be willing to give the angels all of your memories of everything you said, thought, heard, or read today. Release these communications as easily as you dispose of yesterday's newspaper. You don't need them any longer, as they are old news. Allow the angels to take these communications to the light, where they are perfectly purified and returned to you in their pure state of love.

See or feel your throat chakra as an illumined robin's-egg-blue circle, spinning ceaselessly with light and lovingly truthful communication. Our communication channels can become unblocked during our nightly dreams. So let's take a deep breath, and say, "**I ask for and affirm that I will have a dream tonight, which I will remember perfectly, in which any and all blocks to my perfect and Divine communication are forever lifted. I ask for and affirm that all of my karma concerning communication is now balanced in all directions of time.**"

As you become more and more relaxed, ready for a restful night of sleep, affirm, "**I welcome the guidance and lessons during my dreams tonight. I willingly release any fears or reservations that would keep me from enjoying spiritual sight. I ask my angels to help me to see all that is real, true, and from love.**"

Then, with another deep breath, allow your spiritual sense of hearing to become fully open and sensitized to the harmonious sounds of God's wisdom, your angels' love, your higher self's guidance, and the beautiful celestial music from the heavenly spheres. Affirm, "**I receive the word of Love clearly and easily. I enjoy receiving and following the Divine guidance that I hear. My spiritual ears are open, now.**"

Next, see and feel your third eye fully opened as a clear and loving eye in front of you, looking back at you in recognition that you are the same soul in truth. See and feel the chakra colors of dark blue, mixed with sparkles of white and purple light, perfectly aligned, cleansed, and balanced. Affirm: **"It is safe for me to see. I love seeing the beautiful sparkles of my angels' healing light. I trust what I see, knowing that it is always for my highest good."**

As you completely release any remaining tension to the healing holy spirit within you, know that you are fully emerging as the peaceful and loving being whom you are in truth. After a wonderfully refreshing, deep cleansing breath, you are now opening the crown chakra, which is the sky dome of your physical, auric, and etheric body. Take a few deep breaths as you marvel at your eternal connection with all of life.

See and feel your crown chakra as perfectly cleansed and glowing—a violet purple circle at the top of the inside of your head. Affirm: **"I trust and allow a steady inflow and outflow of Divine wisdom to fully enter my conscious-**

ness, now. I love and welcome this Divine guidance, and I intend to seek my higher wisdom in all situations. I deserve good. I deserve love. I deserve success."

You are now ready for a restful, healing sleep filled with wondrous dreams of beauty and uplifting wisdom. See or feel your home completely surrounded with white light, and ask for four guardian angels to be stationed outside of your home throughout the night. It is impossible that any harm could pass by the loving watchfulness of these trustworthy angels. You are safe to let go and relax completely, now. Give thanks to your angels, your higher self, your holy spirit, and to God for all that you are and all that you have. You are ready for a wonderfully restful evening of deep, peaceful, and perfect sleep that will leave you feeling perfectly refreshed and restored in the morning.

Good night. Sweet dreams!

❦

Opening Our Heart Chakras

Earth is ascending. Our consciousness, too, is ascending. We are remembering that we are beings of light and love who are one with everyone and God. Our collective ascension means that our chakras are opening and cleansing. In the 1940s and '50s, Earth's societies worked on overcoming root chakra concerns involving money and security. In the '60s and early '70s, we handled sacral chakra issues about sex, addictions, and other physical appetites. In the 1980s, our thoughts moved through the solar plexus concerns of power and control.

Now, at the turn of the century, our mission is clear. We need to collectively work through our fears of love so that we can fully cleanse and open our heart chakras. The earth's heart chakra is opening right now, lifting her to the frequency level of pure Divine love. Once the earth's heart chakra is fully open, anything unloving cannot remain on the planet. The earth's frequencies simply will not support anything born of fear.

As lightworkers, our primary purpose is to heal ourselves so that we may heal others. When we open our heart chakras fully to Divine love, other people notice the glow that naturally emanates from deep within us. Even those with no knowledge of spirituality are drawn to our love and light. They notice something "different" about our peaceful nature, and the glow of Divine love triggers a deep, forgotten memory of God. So, the greatest mission that lightworkers can now embark upon is to lose the fears of love, so that our light can help to awaken our sleeping brothers and sisters.

The heart chakra becomes clogged, shrunken, and dirty from fears associated with love. It seems that every person has suffered pain in a relationship, including romantic, family, and platonic relationships. This pain causes us to fear love. Yet, because love is the essence of life, this fear causes us to lose touch with life's true essence. We become confused and forget what true love feels like. When we are afraid of love, we are literally afraid of being ourselves.

The fear of love leads us to become guarded, sarcastic, and defensive. We are so frightened of being hurt, manipulated, abused, or controlled that we seal our heart away from all experiences of receiving or giving love. Unfortunately, when we close our hearts to love, we also shut off the awareness of God speaking through our intuition. Ironically, this intuition is the trustworthy guide that reliably leads us to relationships that honor and support us. When we block the awareness of Divine guidance, we are unaware of the angels' warnings about abusive relationships.

Here is a powerful healing meditation given to me by the angels to help us lose our fears about love and cleanse and open our collective heart chakra. You may want to tape-record this meditation, with soft background music, so that you can easily listen to it once or twice a day:

HEART CHAKRA MEDITATION

With your eyes closed, and in a comfortable position, take two or three very deep cleansing breaths. Visualize a beautiful cloud of emerald-green light surrounding you. As you breathe in, you take this healing energy into your lungs, your cells, and your heart. Concentrate on your heart a moment as you allow the emerald-green light to cleanse away any negativity that may have caused you to feel pain.

With a deep breath, allow the light to carry away any fears you may have about love. Be willing to release the fear of feeling love. You need do nothing else except breathe, and hold the intention to heal yourself of the fear of love. Just be willing to be healed, and God and the angels will do everything else. Take another deep breath, as you become willing to release the fear of being loved, including the fear that if you are loved, you could be manipulated, tricked, used, abandoned, rejected, persecuted, or in other ways hurt. With another deep breath, allow all these fears from any lifetime to be lifted and carried away.

Now, allow the light to cleanse you of any fears you may have about giving love. With a deep breath, be willing to release the fear that if you give love, you could be controlled, abused, deceived, betrayed, maimed, or hurt in any way. Allow these fears to be lifted completely, and feel your heart expanding to its natural loving state.

Allow yourself to release any old unforgiveness you may be harboring toward those who seem to have hurt you in a love relationship. Become willing to release unforgiveness toward your mother...toward your father... toward other parental figures...toward your siblings...toward your childhood friends...toward your adolescent friends...toward your first love...toward those whom you dated and loved...toward anyone with whom you lived or married...allow all of your hurts and disappointments associated with love to be cleansed and fully carried away. You don't want the hurt, you don't need it, and with another deep breath, it is lifted to the light where it is transmuted and purified. Only the lessons and the pure essence of love contained within each relationship remains, since that is the only thing that was ever eternal and real within each of your relationships.

Now, with another deep breath, allow the light to cleanse you completely. Be willing to release any unforgiveness you may hold toward yourself connected to love. Be willing to forgive yourself for betraying yourself, for ignoring your intuition, or for not looking out for your highest interests. Give yourself a hug, either in your mind or with your arms. Reassure your inner self that you will never again engage in self-betrayal.

You now commit to following your intuition and discernment so that you could never be or stay in any relationship that would hurt you. Fully release the unforgiveness for any mistakes that you think you may have made in any relationship, including your relationship with yourself. And with another very deep cleansing breath, feel yourself healed, whole, and ready to enjoy the love that is the truth about who you really are.

Chapter Three

Visualizations to Clear Your Chakras

*I*n addition to meditation, your inner vision can clear and balance your chakras. Visualizations work as a great adjunct to meditation, or as a replacement. I often use visualizations when I need to clean my chakras in a hurry, such as right before an unscheduled healing session.

Here are seven visualizations that I find particularly effective:

1. White Light

In your mind's eye, see a large beam of bright, crystal-white light coming into the top of your head. Make the light as bright as you can imagine, like dozens of halogen lightbulbs.

See the light penetrating the inside of the top of your head, clearing away any darkness or dimness from your chakras: the crown at the top of your head, your ear chakras at the sides of your head, your third eye between your two physical eyes, your throat chakra, heart chakra, solar plexus chakra behind your navel, your sacral chakra a few inches below your navel, and your root chakra at the base of your spine.

With your mind's eye, watch as all of the chakras become illuminated and perfectly balanced in size.

2. Glass Globes

Visualize eight beautiful glass globes stacked on top of one another. The globes are stacked from top to bottom:

— Royal purple
— Red-violet
— Deep blue
— Sky blue
— Emerald green
— Sunshine yellow
— Vivid orange
— Ruby red

See the globes become larger, brighter, and increasingly illuminated with light. Make them all grow in size until they are equally large. See the globes as perfectly transparent and the colors as clear, without any spots on the glass.

3. Vacuuming

Picture a giant vacuum tube coming from heavenly clouds. This vacuum is designed to suction away all dark, negative energy. Visualize the vacuum tube going into your head, through your crown chakra at the top of your head. Decide whether to put the vacuum on low, medium, high, or extra-high speed. You can direct the vacuum to suction darkness out of specific places in your chakras. Or, you can ask the vacuum to do a complete cleansing of your entire physical and light body.

4. Breathing Colors

As you take a very deep breath, visualize yourself breathing in the color green. As you exhale completely, see yourself breathing out the color yellow. Next, breathe in the color blue as deeply as you can, and breathe out the color orange. Then, draw in the color purple with your breath, seeing the purple entering all of your cells and your bloodstream. Finally, breathe out the color red completely. Repeat this entire process three times.

5. *Flying Through the Grids*

Imagine yourself in the astral plane, flying around. The sky is draped behind you like deep blue velvet, with sparkling stars. In and around you are glowing grids of intersecting bars that look like neon bars of colored lights. The grids form the shape of open squares, which you can easily fly through.

See yourself jumping toward a grid of glowing red. As you fly nearer to the red bars of light, you hear their sound of electrical pulsations. Flying through the grid, you feel all of your lower-self issues related to money, security, and career scraped away by the pulsating red bars of light.

You then decide to fly over to some bright orange grids, and as you fly through a brightly lit square, you feel all of your body issues being left behind. You turn and see that all of your worries and concerns about your body, including any addictions, are hanging over an orange box through which you just flew. All your issues about your physical body are now cleared away.

With a giant sigh of relief, you then find yourself flying through a beaming yellow grid of bars. You see and feel the yellow lights removing any remaining fears and issues you may have about power or control. Like a giant doormat, the lights scrape away all sediment and weight from your soul.

You next fly in and around beautiful glowing green grids. You have fun repeatedly circling the pulsating squares, marveling at your flying abilities. As you fly through each green square, feel your heart swell with the warmth of universal love. Watch as the green grids scrape away any fears you have about being loved or giving love.

Feeling so alive and great, you then fly between pulsating light blue grids. You hear celestial music emanating from these light blue squares, and you feel like singing. As you join your voice, with great gusto, with the music of the light blue grids, you feel your throat completely open to the joy of expressing yourself fully.

You tumble in a gleeful somersault as you next fly over to some cobalt blue grids that attract your attention. The beauty of the electric blue bars against the velvety night sky takes your breath away. You circle in and through the cobalt blue grids, feeling all of your blocks to clairvoyance scraped away by the magnetic force of the blue squares. You put your face very, very close to one of the cobalt blue bars, and you immerse yourself in looking at the beautiful deep shade of blue. The blue pulsates in a steady beat of one, one, one, and you feel your third eye opening fully in response to the pulsations.

You look around, and the colors in the sky seem even more vivid than ever. You notice a violet-red grid group over to your right, and you fly over to see it. The violet-red grids sing a harmonic tone that sounds like the music of angels cooing and humming. As you fly through the squares, you become aware that your sense of hearing is extremely acute. You hear every tone, every note of the celestial music in this grid group, and you give thanks

that your spiritual sense of hearing is now
fully awakened.

With joy, you fly around and around until
a group of royal purple grids catches your
eye. The deeply bright purple colors, glowing
in neon bars, are breathtaking. You immediately fly over to the purple grids and fly
through the squares. You notice yourself feeling lighter and lighter, better and better, as if
you were regaining a sense of peace and freedom that you hadn't felt in years.

Feeling absolutely wonderful, you fly back
to the earth, back to your country, back to
your city, and back to your home. You open
your eyes and stretch your arms. You feel
great, very alive, and spiritually supercharged.

6. Healing Temple

Closing your eyes and taking some very
deep breaths, visualize two beings of glowing
white light standing before you. These lightbeings love you very much, and you feel their

unconditional, nonjudgmental love pouring over you. They know who you are, and you know who they are.

They take you by the hand, and you willingly allow them to guide you. You look down and notice that the three of you are hovering in the air. The scene of the room you were in has disappeared. Now, you see only the two lightbeings. You look down and notice that you are wearing a glowing white gown. It is the most comfortable, natural-feeling outfit you've ever worn.

You find yourself in a beautiful dome-shaped temple. The lightbeings guide you to stand on an elevated, circular platform. You notice that arched windows surround the top of the temple. Each window has a glass pane with a different jewel-toned color. Just then, a strong beam of light streams through the red glass window, and you see that you are covered with the red light.

The lightbeings ask you to inhale deeply. Then, as you exhale, the stream of light filters through the next window, and you are covered with its reflection of orange light. The lightbeings direct you to turn slowly in a clockwise direction so that your entire body is covered with orange light. When you finish turning in the circle, the beam of light streams through a bright yellow window. Your body glows like the sun's yellow, and you feel warm and loved.

Next, the light streams through a green window, and you marvel at your hands glowing in a bright shade of green. Just then, the beam filters through a light blue window. You are bathed in a gorgeous shade of blue that reminds you of a crystal-clear lake. The lightbeings remind you to keep breathing in and out very deeply. As you do this, the bright light shines through a royal blue window. Your body is blanketed in this deep shade of blue, and you marvel at how magical your gown looks in the glowing light.

The stream of light next filters through a violet-red arched window, and you feel yourself lifted with the strong energy of this colored light that surrounds you. The light then streams brightly through a purple window, and you suddenly hear music fill the temple. You and the lightbeings look up and see hundreds of cherub angels floating around you. They smile with sweet love at you, and you smile broadly back at the cherubs. The light surrounds the temple, shining through all of the windows simultaneously. You watch as a rainbow of jewel colors swirls around the angels, the lightbeings, and yourself.

The lightbeings outstretch their hands and escort you from the elevated platform. You notice how light and wonderful you feel as the lightbeings guide you back into your room. As you open your eyes, you know that you have just received a most rejuvenating treatment in the temple of healing.

7. *Third Eye Opener*

Visualize a glowing golden-white light surrounding you. Breathe in this golden-white light until the inside of your head is completely filled with the light. Exhale, and with another deep breath, see the golden-white light gather like a thick, solid rope. See and feel the rope of golden light go through your third eye. See and feel this rope of light thread through your eye, going from the inside of your head, out into the room. Breathe in and take the rope of light back into your mouth, and feed it through your third eye again.

You may feel a tinge of pressure as your third eye is cleansed and opened by this rope of light. If your third eye has been closed for many years or lifetimes, the rope may feel uncomfortable. Breathe in and out to ease any discomfort during this chakra-opening process.

When you feel guided to stop, visualize yourself exhaling the golden-white light into the room. See your third eye's eyelid joyfully open, happy to be fully awake to the true visions that now guide you.

Chapter Four

Angel Therapy to Clear Your Chakras

*Y*our guardian angels and other members of the angelic realm are happy to help you release the effects of negative and fearful thinking. After all, the angels' purpose is to bring your consciousness to the realization of God's love. So, it is their great pleasure to help you clear away the residue of anything that blocks your awareness of love.

You always have angels around you, nonstop and guaranteed. Despite *anything* you've ever said, thought, or done, the angels love you unconditionally. There are no exceptions to this, and as you read this paragraph, your angels are by your side, right now.

You can call additional angels to your side anytime you like. Simply think, say, or write, "Angels, please come to my side now," and they are with you before you can finish the sentence.

Here are some powerful ways to work with the angels in clearing away the effects of fear:

ANGEL BUCKETS MEDITATION

This is a wonderful meditation to use any time you feel worried about some life challenge. Begin by taking a deep breath.

In your mind's eye, visualize that angels have placed a large bucket in front of you. The angels stand beside the bucket, and they ask you to put anything that is bothering you inside of it.

See and feel yourself placing any worries you may have about money, career, home, or possessions into the bucket. Next, put any concerns you have about your body or health into the bucket. Then, place any conflicts you've had with anyone into it. Follow this with any feelings of hurt you have had in any relationship.

Next, put any guilt or self-recrimination into the bucket. Put it all in. Then, place any fears you may have about your goals into the bucket. Put any fear of failure, or of success, into the bucket. Place any fears that you are an "unqualified imposter" into the bucket. Follow this with any fears you may have about the future. Then, take any hurt feelings or anger you may have toward members of organized religion into the bucket. Next, place any resistance you may have felt toward God into the bucket.

If there's anything else bothering you, please place it into the bucket now. Hold nothing back. Put it all into the bucket now. Notice how light your soul and body feel.

Watch as the angels smile at you as they fly away carrying the bucket. They take all of your worries to the Divine source of all creativity and infinite intelligence. Here, all of your challenges are worked out perfectly.

Everything is resolved in a win-win manner, and you receive perfect solutions easily and harmoniously. Give thanks to God and the angels for this help. Accept their help now, knowing that you deserve it. Know that as you heal yourself, so, too, do you heal the world.

About Etheric Cords

The chakras often have "etheric cords" protruding from them. These cords, which look like surgical tubing, extend to chakras in other people with whom we've had relationships.

Etheric cords most commonly extend to our siblings, followed by (in descending order of what is most commonly found) our father, mother, ex-spouse, ex-lovers, current spouse or lover, our house, children, and close friends.

Fear within our relationships forms these cords. The fear may be characterized as co-dependency, attachments, fear of abandonment, or unforgiveness. Etheric cords act like hoses, with energy directed back and forth between both people. Therein lies the problem.

If the person to whom you are attached is having a life challenge, that person will siphon energy from you. He or she will draw upon your energy supply through the etheric cord. You will then feel drained, without knowing why.

Very often, the people you have had sexual relationships with are attached to your sacral chakra. The people with whom you've experienced conflict are attached to your solar plexus. Those whom you grieve over are attached to your heart chakra.

Those with whom you've had painful relationships, or relationships where you carried all the weight, are attached to your shoulders. This is, in my experience, the root cause of shoulder and neck pain.

A female client of mine complained of having multiple life challenges in her finances, health, and love life. I immediately saw that she had many large etheric cords extending from her back and shoulders. I discerned that the cords were attached to her deceased father, with whom she'd had a contentious relationship.

I asked her to be willing to forgive her father as we cut the cords. Simultaneously, I asked her father to be willing to forgive himself, since he was remorseful about his past relationship with his daughter. When both people were completely willing to forgive, the cords parted. My client reported improvements in all areas of her life immediately following our session.

When we are attached to our home or geographical locations, etheric cords extend from the bottom of our feet, into the ground.

I recently worked with a client who said that she wanted to move. However, she complained that her house wasn't selling. I saw that she had many etheric cords extending from the bottom of her feet into the house's foundation.

I explained to my client that her attachment to the home was preventing its sale. With her permission, we cut the cords. Two days later, her house sold at the full asking price.

Cutting cords doesn't mean "I don't love you or care about you anymore." Cord cutting doesn't necessarily lead to breakups or abandoned relationships. It simply means that you are releasing the dysfunctional parts of your relationships. Remember, fear is the opposite of love, and etheric cords (and all attachments) are created from fear.

Some people worry that they may cut cords to their own soul fragments—that is, the parts of themselves that splintered off during traumatic episodes. This is unlikely to occur; however, you can avoid it entirely by holding the intention of only cutting the cords that block you from feeling full joy and energy. Your soul fragment cords will remain uncut by holding this intention.

Or, you can call back your soul fragments and reintegrate yourself by visualizing a shower of white light encircling your body. Mentally ask that all pieces of yourself be completely reunited with your true self. You may see little "you's" bounding toward you, like little beings on rubber bands bungee-jumping in your direction. These little soul fragments will be completely healed of all residual fear or trauma as they reenter you through the white light shower.

Cutting Etheric Cords

There are two main ways to cut etheric cords. The fastest and simplest way is to mentally call Archangel Michael to come to your side and clear away all cords that are draining you. If you are unfamiliar with Archangel Michael, his primary role is to clear away all dark energy. You can ask Archangel Michael to come to your side any time. You can even ask him to live with you permanently. He has the ability (as do we, in truth) to be with everyone simultaneously.

You will notice an immediate increase in energy and peacefulness when you ask Michael to cut your cords.

The second way is to cut the etheric cords yourself, or ask a friend or healer to do it for you. If you do it yourself, simply visualize holding a pair of scissors, a knife, or a sword. See or feel yourself cutting the etheric cords. You can either think about a person to whom you know you are attached and then hold the intention of cutting the cord, or you can hold the intention of cutting all of your cords.

The sensation of cutting your own cords, or those of another person, is palpable. You can feel the thickness and density of the tubing as you cut through it with your sharp instrument. If there is any resistance to cutting the cord, this signals unresolved fears or unforgiveness held toward the person to whom the cord is attached. Here is an affirmation to heal this resistance: "I am willing to release all fear and unforgiveness so that I may experience peace instead of pain."

Clearing with Archangel Raphael

Raphael is the archangel in charge of healing. He exudes a beautiful emerald-green glow, which provides healing energy. You can invite Archangel Raphael to enter your body and clear your chakras of any residual fear. Raphael will spin his green healing light around each chakra and help you to release all anxiety, guilt, or stress related to each chakra.

Simply think or say, "Raphael, please enter my body and clear me of any imbalances or negative energy now," and it is done. You can also ask Raphael to visit a loved one. The angels will never violate God's will, or a person's free will, so your angel invocation on behalf of another is a pure gift of love from God, the angels, and yourself.

Chapter Five

Additional Methods to Clear Your Chakras

*I*n addition to the methods spelled out in previous chapters, there are dozens of ways to clear your chakras. In fact, the more you clear them, the more creative you will become with methods that you will discern from your own inner guidance. Truly, there is no one "right" way to clear chakras. There are only methods that are right for *you* at any given moment.

So, experiment with creating variations on the methods outlined in this book. Or, ask your guide, "Please show me how to increase my feelings of energy and joy," and then follow whatever positive insight you receive.

I say "positive" because guidance from your guides is always voiced in positive terms. If you ever receive negative guidance, do not follow it, because it is from the lower ego-self and not Divinely originated.

In this chapter, I'll describe a few other methods that open up the chakras.

Toning and Chanting

In ancient times, people would chant the name of the sun god of Thebes, "Amen" or "Amon." They believed that this sun god brought visions of the future. Then, the Egyptian high priestesses and high priests discovered that it was not a pagan god who brought clairvoyant images, but the toning of the name "Amen."

They used the base word *Aum* as a tone to open the third eye. Aum is the sound of creation, and it expresses awe at the miracle of creation and our Creator.

If you chant all three syllables: *Au-Uh-Mm* slowly and loudly, you will feel a strong vibration between your two physical eyes. These pulsations reawaken the third eye's natural ability to see clairvoyantly.

It's even more powerful to chant the Aum tone following sacred numerology. So, chant the tone one, three, or twelve times, and notice the increase in visual imagery. You'll see visions of the future, of the truth about other people, and prophetic dreams.

Forgiveness

Here is an exercise that I ask all of my spiritual counseling students to complete. They always report to me that this exercise substantially increases the clarity and volume of their intuition. This is an extremely powerful way to open up any blocked or shrunken chakras, and I highly recommend it.

Anyone can feel more at peace and more energized through the process of forgiveness. This process reminds me of throwing off weights when riding in a hot air balloon so you can go higher up. Old anger, fear, and resentment are dead weights that slow us and drain our vitality. Perhaps you have some weight you can throw over the side of your hot air balloon right now. When you forgive the world—including yourself—you become lighter and much less fearful.

FORGIVENESS: FREE YOURSELF NOW

This process takes between 30 and 60 minutes to complete, and believe me, it is a worthwhile time investment. Many clients report that this single exercise immediately transforms their lives in powerfully positive ways. Here are some steps to freedom through forgiveness:

1. *Know the benefits of forgiveness.* Forgiveness is different from saying, "I lose," or "I was wrong and you were right." It is different from letting someone off the hook for a perceived

wrong. Forgiveness is simply a way of freeing your spirit and becoming an unlimited being. Peacefulness and increased energy are the prizes, and forgiveness is the price. To me, it's a bargain.

2. *Take a forgiveness inventory*. (This exercise is partially based on the work of author John Randolph Price.) Write the name of *every* being, living or deceased, who has irritated you. Most people find they have a three- or four-page list and are able to suddenly remember names of people they hadn't thought about in years. Some people even put down names of pets who irritated them, and almost everyone writes their own name somewhere on the list.

3. *Release and forgive*. In a solitary room where no interruptions are possible, go down the list one name

at a time. Hold the image of each person in your mind and tell him or her, "I forgive you and I release you. I hold no unforgiveness back. My forgiveness for you is total. I am free and you are free." This process may take 30 minutes or longer. However, it's important to stick with it until the entire list is complete.

4. ***Do nightly releasements***. Every evening before retiring, do a mental review of the day. Is there anyone you need to forgive? Just as you probably wash your face every night, it's also important to cleanse your consciousness nightly so resentment won't accumulate.

Past-Life Clearing of the Third Eye

I've worked with many clients and students who complain that they cannot see images in their mind's eye. They tell me, "I'm just not visual!" Quite often, I find that these seemingly "nonvisual" people have suffered violent deaths in other lives *because of their clairvoyant abilities*.

I've worked with students who were burned at the stake during witch hunts, who were beheaded for possessing psychic abilities during the Inquisition, and who died in the ancient civilization of Atlantis for reasons related to their clairvoyance. Now, in this lifetime, they are terrified of reawakening the very power that led to their demise in past lives.

Similarly, there have been repercussions for many of my psychic students and clients in this lifetime. For instance, they were reprimanded for having "evil" visions as a child. Or, they were told to stop talking about their "invisible friends," who were actually angels or spirit guides.

No matter which lifetime sparked the present fear of clairvoyance, we can heal the resistance simultaneously. Here is a meditative method to clear away the fear of opening your psychic chakras:

Begin by breathing in and out deeply, three times. Read this paragraph to yourself, either aloud or silently, "I am willing to release any fears I may have from any lifetime about being able to see the future. I am willing to release any fear I may have in any direction of time, connected to psychic abilities. I am willing to forgive anyone, in any lifetime, who may have criticized, persecuted, abandoned, maimed, or killed me because of my psychic abilities. I am willing to forgive myself for all the choices I have made in any time, knowing that I was always doing the best I could do. I am willing to release any fears about being harmed for being a psychic in this lifetime. I am healed and I am safe."

The Role of Food and Diet

Everything we eat or drink contains life-force energy, some foods and beverages more than others. If you eat a diet that is high in life-force energy, your chakras will be larger and clearer.

Conversely, a diet that is low in life-force energy doesn't help your chakras, and sometimes makes them shrink and darken even further. This particularly happens whenever we eat foods derived from mistreated animals. Our chakras absorb the energy of the animals' pain.

Foods that are alive, such as fresh fruits and vegetables; sprouted whole grain products; and freshly squeezed (within 20 minutes) juices, have the highest amount of life-force energy. Foods that are dead; or dried, frozen, or overcooked, have no life-force energy. After all, life doesn't live in a can or a freezer.

If you can add more life-force energy to your diet, you'll notice a positive difference in your energy and mood levels. Even cutting back a little bit on low life-force foods and adding a tiny amount of high life-force foods can positively affect you.

I've found that many of my students and clients have received intuitional guidance to stop consuming the foods that clog their chakras. When you give up such foods as sugar, caffeine, or red meat—in response to internal guidance—you will have few or no negative side effects. So, you won't experience the cravings or headaches normally associated with dietary changes. Instead, you'll find that your appetite for these substances disappears.

Here are the foods that affect your chakras most profoundly.

FOODS AND SUBSTANCES THAT NEGATIVELY AFFECT THE CHAKRAS

Greatly:

Alcohol

Caffeine

Chocolate

Cigarettes/cigars

Drugs of any kind

Red meat

Any food or substance consumed compulsively or addictively (this is a sign that Divine guidance is being feared and avoided by the consumption of substances).

Moderately:

Fowl (turkey, chicken, etc.)
Mood-altering or energy-altering herbs
    (calming or stimulating)
Most processed foods
White flour
White sugar

Somewhat:

Carbonation in beverages, including water
Dairy products
Produce and grains grown with pesticides
Seafood (all varieties)

FOODS AND BEVERAGES THAT POSITIVELY AFFECT THE CHAKRAS

- Freshly picked fruits and vegetables (especially those that are organic, as pesticides contain the low life-force energy of death—pesti [insect] cide [death])

- Bread products baked with sprouted or whole grains (ask your grocery store manager to order these, or purchase them at any health food store)

- Soy products such as soy milk or tofu

- Juice, consumed within 20 minutes of squeezing (the life-force escapes after 20 minutes, much like a spirit leaving a body)

Exercise

Exercise also affects the chakras. Any kind of aerobic workout that gets you breathing in and out deeply will aerate your chakras with the increased oxygen flow. Nature walks are also superb for opening your chakras. If you walk in a "power center," such as near a large body of water, a forest, or a vortex (such as the energy vortices in Sedona, Arizona), you will especially feel the impact of your chakras opening.

In addition, yoga and tai chi movements increase the flow of "chi" or life-force through your chakras. I especially like the exercises described in the book *Fountain of Youth* by Peter Kelder (Doubleday). Kelder's book outlines six exercises, purportedly from India, which open the chakras. The exercises definitely open them rapidly.

Crystals

Hold a crystal, such as amethyst, clear quartz, rose quartz, spectrolite, or sugalite, over each chakra. Feel the crystal's fine vibration loosen any hardened fear energy from the chakra. If you breathe deeply and tune in, you may feel the sensation of the crystal's pulsations.

You can also place a crystal under your pillow, on your nightstand, or under your bed, and allow your chakras to be cleared while you sleep.

Some practitioners recommend taking a bath in which crystals are placed in the water. Other healers advise drinking gem elixirs— that is, finely ground crystal or gem powder mixed into distilled water and then consumed.

Massage

Therapeutic massages increase the flow of chi energy and release darkened spots from the chakras. It's best to have a massage in a tranquil environment, such as a dim room with quiet background music. Try to work with a massage therapist who has a pleasant demeanor. Otherwise, you may inadvertently absorb his or her negative energy.

If *you* are a massage therapist, you are probably aware that the chakras in your hands and arms absorb the negative energies released from your clients during a massage. I have clairvoyantly seen this negative-energy effect in my massage therapist clients; it appears as if they are wearing long black gloves.

You can deter this effect by placing several live plants near your arms while you work. The plants absorb the negative energy, much like they absorb carbon dioxide. The plants transmute the negative energy and extract the core of love contained within everything.

Flower Essences and Aromatherapy

The fragrances of certain flowers open the chakras. For instance, pink roses open the heart chakra, and stargazers and tuberoses open the third eye and crown chakras. You can derive these benefits from having the actual flowers nearby (I keep stargazers in my office and next to my bed always), or by using flower essence vials.

Chapter Six

Chakra and Aura Scanning

*D*uring the guided meditations, you saw and felt your chakras. You noticed their size and saw whether they had areas that glowed with white light or were darkened by negativity. We call this "chakra scanning," and it is not your imagination. You *really saw* your chakras in your mind's eye.

As you get into a consistent habit of daily chakra clearing, your spiritual sight will open further. You will see the energy centers within yourself and other people. Your clairvoyance will allow you to see others' "true colors," or their auras.

Chakra Scanning Another Person

You can scan another person's chakras in several ways:

Partner Exercise—Sit face-to-face with a partner. Your eyes can be closed or open, depending on which feels most comfortable and natural. Hold the intention of looking inside their body, scanning for chakras.

If you try too hard to see, or if you hold a fearful intention such as, "I hope I don't make a mistake or a fool of myself," your fear will block your ability to see. Let the images come to you; don't feel that you have to chase them or "make" anything happen. Remember, clairvoyance is an inborn ability that we all have.

Then, look for disks of primary colors of the chakras: red, orange, yellow, green, blue, and purple. See the red disk at the base of your partner's spine, and the other colors in disks vertically atop one another.

If your partner's chakras appear in different sizes or if they are very small (the size of a grapefruit is considered a small chakra), then ask your partner if you can increase their size. After obtaining your partner's permission, visualize the chakras increasing in size until they are uniformly large. Make the largest chakra double in size, and then make the other chakras match this size. Chakras can exceed the body's outline in size.

Next, visualize a beam of white light cleaning each chakra. You can direct the white light, with your intention, to clean each chakra one by one. Keep going until each chakra glows, from the inside, with white light.

Even though you may wonder if you are merely imagining that you are seeing another person's chakras, let me assure you that it is very real. I had a powerful confirmation of the reality of chakra scanning recently.

I was getting ready to have a session with my client, Gloria. During each of our previous sessions, I'd scanned and then cleansed Gloria's chakras. Each time we'd begun our sessions, Gloria's chakras were somewhat dirty.

I fully expected that our impending session would be like no other. So I began the session by asking Gloria to take a deep breath. I find that when a person breathes deeply, I can easier see their chakras and issues.

Still holding the expectation of finding dirty chakras, I was pleasantly shocked to find Gloria's chakras—in fact, her entire body and aura—sparkling clean! I looked all around inside her body, but couldn't find a spot of dirt.

"Gloria, you look great! What have you been doing?" I asked her.

"Oh, I've been using your chakra tape morning and night for the past month," she replied. Her chakra-cleansing routine had cleared Gloria of all psychic residue, and confirmed to me that our chakra scanning is not a product of our expectations—since I had expected to find dirty chakras—or our imaginations. This is real—very real and powerful.

Remote Viewing—You can see the status of any person's chakras even when the person isn't near you physically. Simply close your eyes, take a deep breath, and visualize the person. Hold the intention of seeing inside the person's body and looking at their chakras. You will see glimmers of colored disks inside the person's body. Use your intention and will to brighten and sharpen the colors so that you can clearly see the chakras. Then, mentally ask the person for permission to clear and balance their chakras. If you intuitively get a *yes* answer, continue with adjusting and cleaning the chakras (see the *Partner Exercise* on page 92).

If you receive a *maybe* answer, hold a mental conversation with the person. Usually, you'll find that they are afraid, and you can assuage these fears. If you get a firm *no* reply, then you will need to decide whether to proceed. Some people believe that conducting healings without permission creates karmic imbalances, while others liken it to saving a drowning man even if he refuses help.

Seeing Auras

There is an old story about clairvoyant healer Edgar Cayce that powerfully illustrates the value of seeing auras. Cayce was about to get on an elevator, but then he noticed that no one on the elevator had an aura. Upon seeing this, Cayce decided against entering. Moments later, the elevator malfunctioned, and it plunged to the bottom, injuring many people. Cayce knew that people without auras are headed toward death or serious challenges.

Although your experiences with seeing auras aren't likely to be so dramatic, you will receive great insights into your relationships with others through this ability. The more you work on opening your third-eye chakra, the easier it is to see the energy field, or aura, around other people.

Auras look like the wavering energy field around the sun. They are constantly shifting in size, shape, and coloring, in perfect unison with the person's thoughts and emotions.

You can easily learn to interpret the meaning of auras by studying the chart that follows. This information will help you in all situations, such as knowing if a partner has high integrity, seeing the natural healing ability within a therapist, and viewing a family member's state of mind.

To see an aura, allow your eyes to soften their focus. Hold the intention of seeing the aura, and use your inner vision to discern the colors you see. The aura surrounds a person's body like a cocoon of different colors lying flush against the body shape. However, if a person has a rainbow-colored aura, the stripes of color will emanate vertically away from the person's body, like rays of sunshine.

Aura colors surround the body like a glowing, colorful outline. You can receive information about a person by noticing the colors and size of their aura. Usually, a large aura means a strong, loving, or spiritual nature. Dim or short auras usually mean fear or constricted energy within an individual.

Here is a general interpretation of each common aura color. You will find that these interpretations are usually accurate. However, it's important to always use your psychic discernment to interpret the meanings of an aura. Just as with dream interpretation, there are countless personal meanings behind each color. You will intuitively know the true meanings of each aura color when you see them.

THE GENERAL MEANINGS OF AURA COLORS

Red
Money worries or obsessions; anger or unforgiveness; anxiety or nervousness

Pink
Bright and light: Joy, love, purity, and compassion; new or revived romantic relationship. Can also indicate clairaudience.
Dark and murky: Immature and/or dishonest nature

Orange

Outgoing social nature, very people oriented; highly sexual nature; currently experiencing stress related to appetites and addictions (food, alcohol, drugs, etc.); can also indicate an extremely creative or artistic person and/or a person of great passion and extremely intense emotions.

Yellow

Light or pale yellow: Emerging psychic and spiritual awareness; optimism and hopefulness; positive excitement about new ideas.

Bright lemon yellow: Struggling to maintain power and control in a personal or business relationship; fear of losing control, prestige, respect, and/or power.

Clear gold metallic, shiny, and bright: Spiritual energy and power activated and awakened; an inspired person.

Dark brownish yellow or gold: A student, or one who is straining at studying; overly analytical to the point of feeling fatigued or stressed; trying to make up for "lost time" by learning everything all at once.

Green

"Electric" bright emerald green: A healer (may be a professional healer, a natural healer, or one who is unaware of his or her healing abilities). "Healing hands" usually have an emerald-green aura around the fingertips. Also indicates a love-centered person.

Dark or muddy forest green (the color has no light or dim lighting): Jealousy; resentment; feeling like a victim of the world; blaming self and others; insecurity and low self-esteem; lack of understanding of personal responsibility; sensitive to perceived criticism.

Blue

Light blue: Intuitive; expressive; truthful; may enjoy a career involving communication.

Bright royal blue: Clairvoyant; highly spiritual nature; generous; on the right path; new opportunities are coming.

Dark or muddy blue: Fear of the future; fear of self-expression; fear of facing or speaking the truth.

Purple

Blue (cobalt) purple: Archangel Michael is standing next to the person.

Clear or bright "electric" purple: In tune with the Divine spiritual realm; enlightenment; clair-cognizance.

Dark or muddy purple: Cry for love and attention.

Reddish violet: Clairaudience (the ability to hear the voice of the higher self, God, the angels, ascended masters, or spirit guides).

White

Purity and truth; angelic qualities.

White sparkles or flashes of white light: Angels are nearby; can also indicate that a person is pregnant or will be pregnant soon.

Rainbows

Rainbow-colored stripes, sticking out like sun-beams from the hand, head, or body: A Reiki healer, and/or a starperson (someone who is in their first incarnation on Earth).

Silver

Bright metallic: Receptive to new ideas; intuitive; nurturing.

Dark and muddy gray: Residue of fear is accumulating in the body, with potential for health challenges. This is especially true if you see gray clustered in specific areas of the body.

Black

Usually indicates long-term unforgiveness (toward self or another) collected in a specific area of the body, which can lead to health challenges; also, entities lodged within a person's aura, chakras, or body; alien implants; past-life hurts lodged in the body; and unreleased grief from abortions if the blackness appears in the ovaries.

Chapter Seven

Clearing the Way

*Y*our true self has boundless energy and crystal-clear intuition. You'll enjoy the benefits of both characteristics by keeping your chakras cleared and balanced.

Any time you notice yourself feeling down for no obvious reason, clear your chakras. Whenever you need a little extra insight before making a big decision, clear your chakras. Before an important meeting, clear your chakras.

As you experience the broad benefits of cleared chakras, you will naturally incorporate this routine into your day. As you've read, chakra clearing doesn't have to take a lot of time. You don't necessarily have to be alone or close your eyes. So, please don't procrastinate doing your chakra clearing just because you have a busy schedule. After all, we can use *extra* clarity during hectic days.

You can use many of the chakra-clearing methods described in this book while brushing your teeth, driving to work, or grocery shopping. Simply hold the intention of clearing your chakras, and it is done.

Like taking a nap, getting a foot rub, or taking a nature walk, chakra clearing is a natural avenue to greater peace, perspective, and vitality. In fact, some of my most powerful chakra-clearing experiences have occurred when I've used them outdoors in a garden, near the beach, or in a meadow clearing.

One day, I had a miracle occur when I cleared my chakras at the beach. My husband, Michael, and I were at a Newport Beach quartz rock jetty called "the wedge." I wanted to sit on the wedge rocks and meditate. We carefully selected a high, flat stone on which to sit, since high surf pounded lower areas of the wedge.

After sitting down, I took several deep breaths with my eyes closed. I visualized a bright, diamond-white light cleansing my chakras. As I enjoyed the beauty of the clear and bright colors of each chakra, I felt heart-swelling gratitude for life. The love I felt for everyone and everything enveloped me in warmth. Simultaneously, I enjoyed the surf spray, which cooled my sun-kissed skin. *Everything is so perfect*, I sighed, as I opened my eyes and stretched.

As Michael and I turned to climb down from our perch, I saw a bright object next to me. It was a bouquet! I marveled at how a fresh bunch of purple orchids and a fuchsia rosebud, tied with a bright pink ribbon, could have escaped our attention as we sat on the rock.

Michael didn't bring the flowers with him, since he was wearing only a thin tank top and shorts, with no place to hide a surprise. There were no other people close to us on the wedge who could have dropped the bouquet. And the flowers were too fresh to have been on the rocks long, especially in the mid-afternoon heat.

As Michael and I walked along the beach with our miracle bouquet, my inner voice explained that the flowers were a heavenly gift to honor my experience of universal love. I also heard, "Happy Birthday, Doreen," which brought a smile to my face, since the next day was my birthday.

I now keep the dried petals of my miracle bouquet in my office as a reminder to stay clear in all ways: my chakras, my intentions, and my love. My prayer is that you will choose to enjoy the benefits of clear living as well!

— Love and Angelic Blessings,
Doreen Virtue

Positive Feedback on Doreen Virtue's *Chakra Clearing* Audiocassette*

Ever since the audiocassette *Chakra Clearing* was first released in mid-1997, I have received many letters and comments from people who regularly listen to the tape. Often, as I walk through a Whole Life Expo or other spiritual gathering place, people stop to tell me anecdotes related to the *Chakra Clearing* tape.

One woman said that whenever she becomes agitated, her little grandson will reach for the tape and say, "Here, Grandma, you need to listen to this." Another woman told me that her mother healed from a seemingly serious illness by listening to the tape twice daily. And singer-songwriter Debbie Voltura said that after first listening to *Chakra Clearing*, she immediately wrote a powerful new song.

Of course, as mentioned throughout this book, you don't need to listen to the tape to attain benefits. Any of the methods described herein can powerfully clear your chakras. In addition, you can tape-record the meditations outlined in this book and make your own personalized chakra-clearing audiocassette. As you read the meditations into a tape recorder, play your favorite music in the background, and add a few affirmations that apply specifically to you and your goals.

Here are some comments from people (printed with their permission) who have had positive results from listening to the *Chakra Clearing* tape:

"While using the tape, I found that I was much more at peace, stayed centered in loving energy, felt more connected to Spirit, could more easily catch myself when slipping into 'fearful ego,' moved through the days more effectively, and slept more peacefully."
— Jamey Collins, LCSW

*"Listening to the morning meditation energizes
my entire being—not just the physical self,
but the etheric self as well."*
— Adona Kaye, DCH

*"I use your chakra tape daily, and I can see
greater development of my third eye."*
— Nancine Meyer

*"When I first used your chakra tape, the first
thing that I noticed is that I slept better."*
— Gary Greene, DCH

*"The tape puts me into a more calm and relaxed
mood as I am performing a ritual bath on my
body of ridding myself of the 'dirt' of the day."*
— Marcia K. Niren

*"Your techniques are simple, yet powerful. I have
discovered a difference in the accessibility of my
intuition and guidance when my chakras are
cleansed and balanced."*
— Marjorie Miles, MFCC

"I immediately noticed more peace and balance in my inner feelings and outer activities, and that has continued. My intuitive/spiritual insights began increasing noticeably right away, also."
— Susan Stevenson, DCH

"In just this last three months of meditating with the Chakra Clearing tape, I am able to see my angels and hear louder the Divine guidance of my purpose."
— Mary Lynn Marsico-Foley, RN, BSN

"I have lost weight without any effort since I began listening to the tape."
— Sharon Wilson

*To order the *Chakra Clearing* audiocassette or the hardcover version of *Chakra Clearing*, which includes a CD, please call Hay House at (800) 654-5126, ext. 0.

About the Author

Doreen Virtue, Ph.D., is a clairvoyant/clairaudient metaphysician who holds Ph.D., M.A., and B.A. degrees in psychology. The daughter of a spiritual healer, Doreen is a life-long student of metaphysics. She works with the angelic realm in her healing, teaching, and writing work.

Doreen gives angel readings to random audience members during her workshops, which are conducted across the country each week. To receive her workshop schedule, please call or write Hay House, or visit Doreen's Website at: **www.AngelTherapy.com.**

Hay House Titles of Related Interest

Books

The Experience of God: *How 40 Well-Known Seekers Encounter the Sacred,* by Jonathan Robinson

Experiencing the Soul: *Before Birth, During Life, After Death,* by Eliot Rosen

7 Paths to God, by Joan Z. Borysenko, Ph.D.

Your Personality, Your Health: *Connecting Personality with the Human Energy System, Chakras, and Wellness,* by Carol Ritberger, Ph.D.

All of the above are available at your local bookstore, or may be ordered by visiting:

Hay House USA: **www.hayhouse.com**
Hay House Australia: **www.hayhouse.com.au**
Hay House UK: **www.hayhouse.co.uk**
Hay House South Africa: **www.hayhouse.co.za**
Hay House India: **www.hayhouse.co.in**

Tune in to **HayHouseRadio.com**® for the best in inspirational talk radio featuring top Hay House authors! And, sign up via the Hay House USA Website to receive the Hay House online newsletter and stay informed about what's going on with your favorite authors. You'll receive bimonthly announcements about: Discounts and Offers, Special Events, Product Highlights, Free Excerpts, Giveaways, and more!

www.hayhouse.com®

We hope you enjoyed this Hay House book.
If you would like to receive a free catalog featuring
additional Hay House books and products, or if you would
like information about the Hay Foundation, please contact:

Hay House, Inc.
P.O. Box 5100
Carlsbad, CA 92018-5100

(760) 431-7695 or **(800) 654-5126**
(760) 431-6948 (fax) or **(800) 650-5115 (fax)**
www.hayhouse.com

✍ ✍ ✍

Published and distributed in Australia by: Hay House Australia Pty. Ltd.,
18/36 Ralph St., Alexandria NSW 2015 • *Phone:* 612-9669-4299
Fax: 612-9669-4144 • www.hayhouse.com.au

Published and distributed in the United Kingdom by: Hay House UK,
Ltd., 292B Kensal Rd., London W10 5BE • *Phone:* 44-20-8962-1230
Fax: 44-20-8962-1239 • www.hayhouse.co.uk

Published and distributed in the Republic of South Africa by: Hay House
SA (Pty), Ltd., P.O. Box 990, Witkoppen 2068 • *Phone/Fax:* 27-11-467-
8904 • orders@psdprom.co.za • www.hayhouse.co.za

Published in India by: Hay House Publishers India, Muskaan Complex,
Plot No. 3, B-2, Vasant Kunj, New Delhi 110 070 • *Phone:* 91-11-4176-
1620 • *Fax:* 91-11-4176-1630 • www.hayhouse.co.in

Distributed in Canada by: Raincoast, 9050 Shaughnessy St., Vancouver,
B.C. V6P 6E5 • *Phone:* (604) 323-7100 • *Fax:* (604) 323-2600
www.raincoast.com

✍ ✍ ✍